REMEMBERING SEVEN PROPHETS

Joseph Fielding Smith

MEMORIES OF FRANCIS M. GIBBONS
AS TOLD TO DANIEL BAY GIBBONS

Sixteen Stones Press

HOLLADAY, UTAH

Copyright © 2014 by Daniel Bay Gibbons

All rights reserved. No part of this publication may be reproduced, distributed or transmitted in any form or by any means, including photocopying, recording, or other electronic or mechanical methods, without the prior written permission of the publisher, except in the case of brief quotations embodied in critical reviews and certain other noncommercial uses permitted by copyright law.

Book layout, typography, and cover design ©2015 by Julie G. Gibbons. Photo credits: all cover photographs from the private collection of Francis M. Gibbons, used by permission. Sixteen Stones Press logo design by Marina Telezar.

Sixteen Stones Press
Publisher website: www.sixteenstonespress.com

Joseph Fielding Smith
(Remembering Seven Prophets, Book 1)
by Daniel Bay Gibbons

Paperback ISBN 978-0-9906387-3-5
eBook ISBN 978-0-9906387-2-8

Table of Contents

Remembering Seven Prophets 1

Chronology of the Life of President Joseph
Fielding Smith 5

"A contemporary of fifteen Prophets" 13

"The long shadow of history" 15

"A trunk which had belonged to Hyrum
Smith" 17

"A most distinguished name" 20

"Watching the stone cutters at work on the
temple" 21

"The shadow of persecution" 23

"Much love, but very little money" 26

"We got a scolding from the Prophet" 28

"A defender of the doctrine" 29

"They crossed the Atlantic in a sailing ship" 30

"The most prolific writer of any of the
modern Prophets" 33

"A widower at age thirty-one" 35

"I guess we'll have to sell the cow" 37

"Serving as his father's private secretary" 39

"They built a new family home on Douglas Street" 41

"A lesson on the Word of Wisdom" 43

"An impromptu sermon on the evils of profanity" 45

"Let's go up and watch the football game" 47

"A widower for the second time" 49

"Their unusual courtship" 50

"Fun-loving and full of life" 52

"Awakened by the sound of jackboots" 53

"Bowed down with grief" 54

"Physically vigorous and active" 56

"As excited as a schoolboy to be flying" 57

"My first impressions of the Prophet" 59

"Constantly praying within himself" 62

"One of the kindest men I have ever known" 63

"A delicious sense of humor" 65

"Watch out! Woman driver!" 66

"President Smith is here!" 67

"Who is that woman in your office?" 68

"The firm handshake of a man in his prime" 69

"He never ate meat" 71

"A deep love for the temple" 72

"The next day he was back at his desk" 74

"A widower for the third time" 75

"A quorum of living Apostles on foreign soil" 76

"God be with you, 'til we meet again" 77

"Compensation for a lifetime" 78

"He died peacefully" 79

About the Author 81

Index 81

REMEMBERING SEVEN PROPHETS

This collection of reminiscences about the life of President Joseph Fielding Smith, the tenth President of The Church of Jesus Christ of Latter-day Saints, is part of a larger work entitled *Remembering Seven Prophets*. This work is the fruit of more than eighty hours of interviews I conducted with my father, Francis M. Gibbons, between the years 2001 to 2011, and then another dozen hours of interviews conducted between July and November of 2014 following my return from presiding over the Russia Novosibirsk Mission of the Church.

"A Plutarch to the Presidents of the Church"

Now in his ninety-fourth year, Francis M. Gibbons is perhaps the greatest student on the lives of the Presidents of the Church in this dispensation. He has two unique qualifications to speak and write about the Prophets.

First, over the past forty-five years, my father has become "a Plutarch to the Presidents of the Church." This unusual phrase has reference to Plutarch, the ancient

Greek writer, who became the most famous biographer in history, the "Father of Biography." In 1971 my father shared with my mother his special aspiration to become "a Plutarch to the Presidents of the Church, and through their lives to write the history of the Church." If any man or woman deserves the title "Plutarch to the Presidents of the Church," it is my father, Francis M. Gibbons. Over the past four decades he has become by far the most prolific writer of biographies of the Presidents of the Church, writing a full-length biography of every Prophet from Joseph Smith to Gordon B. Hinckley. Dad's biographies of the Prophets have been very popular, selling many hundreds of thousands of copies. Thirteen of his presidential biographies have been included in Brigham Young University's list of "Sixty Significant Mormon Biographies." He has truly become "a Plutarch to the Presidents of the Church."

"A Scribe to the Prophets"

Second, my father has been a personal witness and observer of the character of the last seven Presidents of the Church: Presidents Joseph Fielding Smith, Harold B. Lee, Spencer W. Kimball, Ezra Taft Benson,

Howard W. Hunter, Gordon B. Hinckley, and Thomas S. Monson. He knew these men personally. He worked with them. While serving from 1970 to 1986 as the secretary to the First Presidency and later as a member of the Seventy, Dad associated with them on a daily basis.

"I am their witness"

When Dad was sustained as a General Authority in April of 1986, after many years serving as the faithful scribe for the Presidents of the Church, he said:

> The Church is led by prophets, seers and revelators. I am their witness. I testify that they are honorable, upright, dedicated men of integrity, committed to teaching the principles of the gospel, who strive with all of their might to prepare a people ready for the return of the head of the Church, Jesus Christ, at His second coming.

This work, *Remembering Seven Prophets*, shares many unique stories, anecdotes, insights, and testimonies about the last seven Presidents of the Church, which are nowhere else available.

REMEMBERING SEVEN PROPHETS

I offer this work for the enlightenment and inspiration of the reader and as a tribute to the memory of the seven Presidents of the Church featured in these pages. I love and honor these great men and add my witness to that of my father that they were and are Prophets of God!

Daniel Bay Gibbons
November 20, 2014
Holladay, Utah

CHRONOLOGY OF THE LIFE OF PRESIDENT JOSEPH FIELDING SMITH

July 19, 1876
Joseph Fielding Smith is born in Salt Lake City to Joseph F. Smith and Julina Lambson Smith.

January 1879
The U.S. Supreme Court issues its decision in *Reynolds v. United States*, which upheld the constitutionality of the Morrill Anti-Bigamy Act of 1862, which had criminalized the Latter-day Saint practice of plural marriage. Joseph Fielding Smith's family is dramatically affected by efforts to arrest and prosecute his father, President Joseph F. Smith.

April 26, 1898
Joseph Fielding Smith is married to his first wife, Louie Shurtliff, in the Salt Lake Temple.

May 13, 1899
Joseph Fielding Smith departs for his mission to England with his older brother, Joseph Richards Smith.

March 30, 1908
Joseph Fielding Smith's first wife, Louie Shurtliff Smith, passes away.

November 2, 1908
Joseph Fielding Smith is married to his second wife, Ethel Reynolds, in the Salt Lake Temple.

April 7, 1910
In a surprise announcement, Joseph Fielding Smith is sustained as a member of the Quorum of the Twelve Apostles. After his call to the Apostleship, he continued to serve as the confidential secretary for his father, Church President Joseph F. Smith.

November 19, 1918
Elder Joseph Fielding Smith's father, President Joseph F. Smith., passes away. One of his last services to his father was to record his vision of the dead, which now appears as section 138 of the Doctrine and Covenants.

1921
Elder Joseph Fielding Smith is appointed as Church Historian.

1922

Elder Joseph Fielding Smith publishes his book, *Essentials in Church History*. He would eventually write more than twenty books.

1925

Elder Joseph Fielding Smith builds a new family home on Douglas Street in Salt Lake City.

August 26, 1937

Elder Joseph Fielding Smith's second wife, Ethel Reynolds Smith, passes away.

April 12, 1938

Elder Joseph Fielding Smith marries his third wife, Jessie Evans, in the Salt Lake Temple

April 21, 1939

Elder Joseph Fielding Smith leaves Salt Lake City for extended tour of European Missions. He would not return home until November of 1939.

July 4, 1939

Elder Joseph Fielding Smith is awakened in Florence, Italy, by the movement of Mussolini's fascist troops.

August 23, 1939
Elder Joseph Fielding Smith oversees the evacuation of all missionaries serving in Germany prior to the outbreak of World War II.

September 3, 1939
Elder Joseph Fielding Smith goes to Copenhagen, Denmark, where he oversees the evacuation of all missionaries serving in Europe.

November 1939
Elder Joseph Fielding Smith returns home after being in Europe for seven months.

March 4, 1942
Elder Joseph Fielding Smith's son Lewis is drafted.

1944
Elder Joseph Fielding Smith delivers two series of radio lectures entitled "The Signs of the Times" and "The Restoration of All Things."

December 29, 1944
Joseph Fielding Smith's son Lewis is killed in action in North Africa.

June 1945
Elder Joseph Fielding Smith is called as President of the Salt Lake Temple.

August 8, 1950
Elder Joseph Fielding Smith is sustained as Acting President of the Quorum of the Twelve Apostles following the death of Elder George F. Richards.

April 9, 1951
President Joseph Fielding Smith is sustained as President of the Quorum of the Twelve Apostles following the death of President George Albert Smith.

September 1958
President Joseph Fielding Smith travels to England and Western Europe for the dedication of the London Temple and special training in the Swiss Temple.

November 1958
President Joseph Fielding Smith travels to the South Pacific for missionary and member meetings.

October 1960
President Joseph Fielding Smith leaves for an extended tour of South America, where he holds meetings in Brazil, Uruguay, Argentina, Chile, Peru, Ecuador, and Guatemala.

November 1963
President Joseph Fielding Smith travels to Australia for missionary and member meetings.

October 29, 1965
President Joseph Fielding Smith is called as additional counselor in the First Presidency.

Summer of 1966
President Joseph Fielding Smith accompanies President David O. McKay for an inspection of Church history sites in Missouri.

January 18, 1970
President David O. McKay passes away.

January 23, 1970

President Joseph Fielding Smith is ordained and set apart as the tenth President of the Church.

August 3, 1971

President Joseph Fielding Smith's third wife, Jessie Evans Smith, passes away.

August 26, 1971

President Joseph Fielding Smith arrives in Manchester, England, for the Church's first Area Conference. The night before the Conference, Joseph Fielding Smith presides at a special Council of the First Presidency and the Quorum of the Twelve, the first such meeting held on foreign soil since 1840.

July 2, 1972

President Joseph Fielding Smith dies peacefully in the home of his daughter, Amelia Smith McConkie, seventeen days before his ninety-sixth birthday.

"A CONTEMPORARY OF FIFTEEN PROPHETS"

President Joseph Fielding Smith might have touched the lives of more Church leaders than any other President of the Church. The grandnephew of the Prophet Joseph Smith, he was a contemporary of the succeeding fifteen Prophets of this dispensation. He was born July 19, 1876, during the lifetime of President Brigham Young. He lived during the lifetime of each of the Presidents of the Church who preceded him except for the Prophet Joseph Smith. As a boy and a young man, he was personally acquainted with Presidents John Taylor, Wilford Woodruff, and Lorenzo Snow. He served in the Quorum of the Twelve during the administrations of his father, President Joseph F. Smith, and then under Presidents Heber J. Grant, George Albert Smith, and David O. McKay. By the time he was ordained as the tenth President of the Church on January 23, 1970, he had personally witnessed nearly a century of Church history. He was also a contemporary of the six Church Presidents who succeeded him after his death (as of November of 2014), having served in the

First Presidency or the Quorum of the Twelve with Presidents Harold B. Lee, Spencer W. Kimball, Ezra Taft Benson, Howard W. Hunter, Gordon B. Hinckley, and Thomas S. Monson.

Thus, President Smith represents a sort of welding link, connecting all Church Presidents, past and present.

"THE LONG SHADOW OF HISTORY"

The long shadow of history hung over Joseph Fielding Smith from the moment of his birth. He had the most unique upbringing of any of the Prophets I had the privilege of working under. He was born, of course, into the most distinguished family in the Church. From his birth, he was surrounded by many who were intimately acquainted with the earliest period of Church history. His father, President Joseph F. Smith, was the son of Hyrum Smith and the nephew of Joseph Smith and had boyhood memories of living in Missouri and in Nauvoo.

President Smith was also very close to his great-aunt Thompson, Mercy Fielding Thompson, who was a plural wife of his grandfather, Hyrum Smith, and was personally acquainted with Joseph and Emma Smith. She was able to share with her grandnephew firsthand impressions of the personalities and perspectives of first-generation Latter-day Saints. He was also personally acquainted with Church Presidents John Taylor, Wilford Woodruff, and Lorenzo Snow, and many of the older Apostles who had been contemporaries of his great-uncle

Joseph Smith, Jr., and his grandfather Hyrum Smith. These associations gave President Smith a special and unusually vivid sense of history.

The sense of history that Joseph Fielding Smith acquired through these relationships was sharpened by the natural inclinations of his mother, Julina Lambson Smith. She was a remarkably intelligent and perceptive woman. Before her marriage to Joseph F. Smith, she had been an employee in the Church Historian's Office. There she acquired a keen interest in Church history and doctrine, which I'm sure she passed on to her son, resulting in his lifelong passion for history.

"A TRUNK WHICH HAD BELONGED TO HYRUM SMITH"

President Joseph Fielding Smith had inherited a very old trunk, which had belonged to Hyrum Smith, and an old safe, which had belonged to his father, President Joseph F. Smith. These had been stored, unopened, for decades in President Smith's home on Douglas Street and later in his apartment in the Eagle Gate in downtown Salt Lake City.

After he became the President of the Church in 1970, President Smith gave the safe to the Church. I was with the Prophet when it was opened and inventoried. As we went through the items, President Smith provided fascinating information about the contents and about his family and personal history.

There were so many things of special historic significance inside this old safe that it was almost overwhelming. It was a special experience to be in the presence of the aged Prophet when these things were brought forth. It gave me a sense of President Smith's deep personal connection to the past. Inside the safe there was a veritable treasure trove of documents, journals, letters, and artifacts of great historical significance to the Smith family and the Church. Among the items in the safe were an old family Bible almost four hundred years old, numerous journals and other documents dating back to the earliest days of the Church, memorabilia from Kirtland and Nauvoo, artifacts related to the martyrdom of Joseph and Hyrum in the Carthage Jail, and many, many other fascinating things.

Upon his death, President Joseph Fielding Smith also bequeathed to the Church the old trunk in his possession. Shortly after the Prophet's death, I accompanied President Smith's sons Joseph and Douglas, President Gordon B. Hinckley, and several others to inspect this old trunk. It had belonged to his grandfather, Hyrum Smith, and was brought across the plains in a covered wagon by his grandmother, Mary Fielding Smith, and his father, Joseph F. Smith. The trunk bore a nameplate with the inscription, "Hirum Smith, Hancock County, Illinois." In it were several items of clothing that had belonged to Hyrum Smith, including his Nauvoo Legion uniform, some personal belongings of Joseph F. Smith, and some miscellaneous old newspapers and other documents. The trunk had not been opened in some time, and it was necessary to get the help of a locksmith before the trunk could be opened.

These experiences seeing and handling these Smith family artifacts, preserved for nearly a century and a half by President Joseph F. Smith and his son, President Joseph Fielding Smith, represent some of the most interesting and inspiring hours I have ever spent in my life.

"A MOST DISTINGUISHED NAME"

Joseph Fielding Smith was a child of great promise and he was given a most distinguished name.

His father, President Joseph F. Smith, had six wives and nearly fifty children. I understand that Joseph Fielding Smith's mother, Julina Lambson, had been promised that her first son would bear his father's full name, Joseph Fielding Smith, even though he had an older brother who was several years older. Like his father, Joseph Fielding Smith was named after the Prophet Joseph Smith. He was also named after his grandmother, Mary Fielding Smith, an early English convert who married Hyrum Smith in Kirtland in 1837. So the name was full of significance, both for the Church and for the young Joseph Fielding Smith personally.

It is interesting that during his early life, he always identified himself as Joseph F. Smith, Jr., but following the death of his father, the Prophet, he began to refer to himself as Joseph Fielding Smith.

"WATCHING THE STONE CUTTERS AT WORK ON THE TEMPLE"

When I first began working with President Smith in 1970, it was almost an everyday occurrence to hear the Prophet speak of matters occurring in the 1880's or 1890's like it was yesterday. He was born in 1876, and so his memory stretched many years before the completion of the Salt Lake Temple. One day I had a sweet conversation with the Prophet as we walked from the Church Administration Building to the temple. He told me about his boyhood and how he would go each summer to Little Cottonwood Canyon with his father, President Joseph F. Smith, to stay in a little rustic cabin the family had there. While in the canyon, he and his father would hike over to watch the quarrymen hew the massive blocks of granite to be transported to Temple Square. He also said that his boyhood home was on 100 North Street, close to Temple Square, and he reminisced with me about how he would often run over to watch the stone cutters at work on the temple. He said that it was fascinating to watch them shape the great stones that were raised in place on the walls and towers. He also mentioned attending the dedication of the Salt Lake Temple in 1893, when he was sixteen years old, and seeing the venerable aged Prophet, President Wilford Woodruff, in his immaculate white suit as he dedicated the sacred building.

"THE SHADOW OF PERSECUTION"

I was privileged to have several conversations with President Joseph Fielding Smith about his boyhood. He remembered his childhood in the 1870's and 1880's with great fondness, despite the difficult circumstances under which his family lived. President Smith grew up under a kind of shadow, which was the heavy anti-Mormon persecution then waged by the federal government against the Church. So his boyhood was happy within the home, but often difficult and traumatic outside. The trauma came from the countless times his father had to leave home to avoid arrest because of his practicing plural marriage. In the late 1870's, when the Prophet was only a toddler, the U.S. Supreme Court issued its opinion, *Reynolds v. United States*, upholding the constitutionality of the Morrill Anti-Bigamy Act. This ruling was a serious blow to the Church and to Joseph F. Smith and many other Latter-day Saints who were then practicing plural marriage. It essentially made criminals of an entire generation of Mormons, and aggressive federal enforcement followed under the Edmunds-Tucker Act. Many Church leaders were imprisoned or forced into hiding and exile in the aftermath of the *Reynolds* case. President Joseph Fielding Smith's father was no exception, and he took President Smith's mother and his younger sister and left for Hawaii, where he lived for about three years. So for a time during his adolescence, President Joseph Fielding Smith was deprived of the companionship of his father as he evaded arrest.

During his father's long absence, President Smith continued to live with his brothers and sisters and his father's other wives in the only family home on 100 North in Salt Lake City. Young Joseph always called his father's other wives "aunties." There was a great deal of affection in that large, unusual family. So Joseph Fielding Smith really lived a life of simple happiness. I'm sure this happiness came principally from being part of an unusually close-knit and unified family consisting of his parents, the "aunties," and many brothers and sisters. Most of the siblings, of course, were half brothers and sisters, but I understand from members of the family that none of the children were ever regarded as a "half-brother" or a "half-sister," and in fact they were offended if anyone ever referred to them as such. In the Smith family, they were all brothers and sisters, without regard to which mother gave them birth.

The shadow of persecution that hung over the family never really lifted until Joseph Fielding Smith was in his mid teens. Even after his father's return from Hawaii, he was unable to openly visit or support his wives and children. This sad state of affairs continued until 1891, when Joseph F. Smith and other Church leaders received a federal pardon from U.S. President Benjamin Harrison.

"Much love, but very little money"

While rich in family heritage, President Joseph Fielding Smith's family was poor in the wealth of the world. President Joseph F. Smith lived very frugally. There was much love, but very little money. He had few opportunities to accumulate money during his lifetime. Almost from his boyhood he was engaged full time in missionary work and Church leadership service.

All members of the family worked to provide means to live. President Joseph Fielding Smith's mother was a midwife, who delivered babies as a way to supplement their income. She became exceptionally skilled at her work as a midwife. It is reported that she delivered nearly a thousand babies in her career without ever having a mother or an infant die in childbirth. Young Joseph Fielding Smith contributed to the family income by becoming his mother's chauffeur, driving her to visit her patients in the family carriage. He had a favorite horse named Meg, and whenever needed, he would hitch Meg up to the carriage. At all hours of the day or night, and in all weather, Joseph made himself available to drive his mother to her work. He also earned money by working in the warehouse at the old ZCMI store carrying heavy boxes and moving goods from one place to another, tasks that resulted in a permanent injury to his shoulder.

There was very little money in the family to provide for an education for the young man. He did attend two years at the old LDS College, after which he began working as his father's secretary, taking dictation, writing letters, and conducting research. It is interesting to contemplate this special relationship of father and son, the President of the Church working side by side with his secretary, who would, in his high old age, also become the President of the Church.

"We got a scolding from the Prophet"

President Smith often recalled an experience he had as a boy when he was scolded by the Prophet. When the Tabernacle Choir sang at the World's Fair in Chicago in the early 1890's, Joseph Fielding Smith was invited to attend and traveled on the train with a group that included President Wilford Woodruff. President Smith would have been about sixteen years old at the time. During the long train trip, he spent much of his time visiting with a son and daughter of President Woodruff, and they became good friends. The three teenagers explored the train and had a grand time together. One day the trio procured a watermelon and took it to the rear of the train, where they sat on the open platform laughing, talking, eating watermelon, and spitting seeds over the low railing onto the tracks behind. Word of this behavior apparently found its way to President Woodruff, and when the teenagers returned to the Prophet's private car, he gave them a good talking to. President Smith said, "We got a scolding from the Prophet!"

"A DEFENDER OF THE DOCTRINE"

Not long before his call to serve as a missionary, when he was about twenty years old, President Joseph Fielding Smith was given a patriarchal blessing by his uncle, John Smith, who was the oldest son of Hyrum Smith. The blessing was remarkable. It essentially laid out the young man's entire life before him.

There were two very significant promises in the blessing. He was told that he would "sit in counsel" with his brethren and "preside among the people." He was also promised that he would "live to a good old age." President Smith ultimately lived to age 95. The only Presidents who surpassed him in age were President David O. McKay, who lived to age 96, and President Gordon B. Hinckley, who lived to age 97.

President Smith's oldest son, Joseph Fielding Smith, Jr., told me that his father had received a second patriarchal blessing after he had been a member of the Twelve for about three years. In it he was promised that he would become preeminent as an expounder of the gospel and as a defender of the doctrine taught by the Prophet Joseph Smith.

"They crossed the Atlantic in a sailing ship"

As an additional means of supporting the family, Joseph's mother, Julina, often took boarders into the large family home on 100 North Street in Salt Lake City. One such boarder was a young woman named Louie Shurtliff, who was a student at the University of Utah, from Ogden, Utah. President Smith fell in love with this girl and began to court her, and the two were married in the Salt Lake Temple in 1898. About a year later, Joseph Fielding Smith was called to serve a mission for the Church in Great Britain. It was quite common in those days to call married men into the mission field. The wives of these missionaries were left to fend for themselves at home, with the help of their families. During President Smith's mission to England, his wife moved back home to Ogden to live with her parents.

President Smith traveled to his field of labor in England with his older brother, Joseph Richards Smith. They crossed the Atlantic in a sailing ship. It is interesting to contemplate that a Prophet who served in the years after men landed on the moon spent his boyhood and young manhood in a world of horses and buggies and sailing ships!

Arriving in Liverpool, young Joseph was assigned by his mission president to serve in Nottingham, England. In Nottingham Joseph first experienced the great derision and hostility then shown towards Mormons in England. A few days after his arrival, while leaving the missionaries' rented room, Joseph and his companion were surrounded by a gang of rowdy English boys who taunted the Elders and sang a parody of a Church hymn, "Chase me girls to Salt Lake City, where the Mormons have no pity." Elder Smith was also shocked at the gross immorality he witnessed, including public drunkenness and immoral acts committed openly in public parks. He said that he saw more wickedness in his first two weeks in England than in his entire life at home.

In England the proselyting activities consisted almost exclusively of door-to-door and street contacting. He did not see much success. After several months, Elder Smith was transferred to Derby, where he served as a senior companion to a man in his thirties. The work in Derby was as unsuccessful as it had been in Nottingham. After a time in

Derby, Elder Smith and his companion were transferred back to Nottingham, where his junior companion was called as the conference president. Elder Smith was now the junior companion. This was a shock, but Elder Smith humbly accepted the junior role. He served as a junior companion the rest of his mission! I'm sure that this experience schooled him in the way of the priesthood. It also prefigured his life of service in the Church. He spent almost his entire life in a junior role. It was only in his high old age that he finally had a chance to preside.

The work in England was very unfruitful during the time of President Smith's service there. Despite all his diligent labors, he did not baptize a single convert during his entire mission.

During his mission he immersed himself deeply in the study of the scriptures and Church history. He reported that even his senior companion, the conference president, deferred to the younger Elder Smith in doctrinal and scriptural matters. He also had the gift of healing, and many people who came to him for blessings were healed of sicknesses.

"THE MOST PROLIFIC WRITER OF ANY OF THE MODERN PROPHETS"

After returning home from his mission, Elder Joseph Fielding Smith was hired as a clerk in the Church Historian's Office. Thus began an association with the Historian's Office that lasted his entire life. Ultimately he served as an assistant historian and then for many decades as the Church historian. When he commenced his service, he worked under Anthon H. Lund, the Church historian, whose assistants were Orson F. Whitney, B. H. Roberts, and Andrew Jenson. All of these men were skilled researchers and writers and became role models for young Joseph Fielding Smith, who soon established himself as a writer. His first published work was entitled *Asael Smith of Topsfield*, which explored the Smith family heritage in New England. This was followed by *Blood Atonement and the Origin of Plural Marriage,* and *Origin of the Reorganized Church and the Question of Succession*. Eventually Joseph Fielding Smith published more than twenty books. He is the most prolific writer of any of the modern Prophets.

In 1921, after his call to the Apostleship, he became the Church Historian, leading the office in which he had worked for twenty years, since his return home from his mission to England. In 1922, his book *Essentials in Church History* was published, which became one of the most popular works of history ever published in the Church, going through dozens of editions and being translated into many foreign languages.

"A WIDOWER AT AGE THIRTY-ONE"

Joseph Fielding Smith and his wife Louie built a small home in Salt Lake City and became the parents of two daughters. Their names were Josephine and Julina. Joseph was soon called to the Salt Lake Stake high council and as a member of the Young Men's General Board.

Then, his life was shattered when his wife Louie passed away suddenly in early 1908 from pregnancy-related complications. Joseph was suddenly a widower at age thirty-one, with two little daughters.

Into this family tragedy stepped Joseph's kindly and loving father, President Joseph F. Smith, then President of the Church. The Prophet invited his son to move into the Beehive House, then the official residence of the President of the Church, where the motherless daughters would have care while their father pursued his work in the Church Historian's Office.

Within a few months after the death of Joseph's young wife, his father tactfully, but clearly, suggested that he ought to remarry, and for the sake of the little orphaned girls, remarry soon.

Working in the Church Historian's Office was a young woman, Georgina Ethel Reynolds, who was the daughter of Elder George Reynolds, a former assistant secretary to the First Presidency, and then a member of the First Council of Seventy. Elder Reynolds had been the plaintiff in a court case against the United States government challenging the constitutionality of the Federal anti-Mormon legislation. The case *Reynolds v. United States* had made Ethel's father famous among Latter-day Saints. Joseph began to court Ethel discreetly. They were married in the Salt Lake Temple on November 2, 1908. Ethel became a loving mother to little Josephine and Julina, and life returned more or less to normal for President Smith and his young family.

"I GUESS WE'LL HAVE TO SELL THE COW"

In 1910 Joseph Fielding Smith's life was again turned upside down. While sitting in General Conference, with no advance notice whatsoever, he heard his name presented as a member of the Quorum of the Twelve Apostles. He was only thirty-three years old. In many ways, this event altered his life far more than the death of his wife two years earlier. Things would never be the same for the young man and his family.

His comment to his wife after his surprising new call was, "Well, I guess we'll have to sell the cow!"

He approached the calling humbly and prayerfully, despite immediate opposition. Shortly after he was sustained, the anti-Mormon newspaper, *The Salt Lake Tribune*, published a vicious editorial entitled, "The Church of the Smiths," which criticized the calling of the Prophet's young son to the Apostleship. The Tribune pointed out that seven of the Church's twenty-seven General Authorities were members of the Smith family. It accused the Prophet of "Smith-i-sizing the Mormon Church," then went on to paint the

Church and its President and his family in words of mockery and disdain.

As a member of the Quorum of the Twelve, Joseph Fielding Smith traveled almost every week, often under difficult circumstances. He went by railway and by horse and carriage, even reaching remote Mormon communities in the American west on horseback. He invariably stayed with local Church leaders rather than in hotels.

In his early years of apostolic service, he developed a pattern for speaking which would remain with him throughout his life. He tried to preach pure doctrine from the scriptures. He developed a reputation for speaking boldly and directly about many subjects. Though his sermons could be quite stern, away from the pulpit he was filled with good humor and kindness. He also liked to have fun, and during conference visits he would often participate in athletic competitions with the young men in outlying communities.

"SERVING AS HIS FATHER'S PRIVATE SECRETARY"

After his call to serve as an Apostle, Joseph Fielding Smith continued serving as his father's private secretary. His father, President Joseph F. Smith, of course, was then the President of the Church. He continued in this special assignment from 1910 until the Prophet's death in 1918. It was a blessing to his father to have a son serving by his side. Young Joseph Fielding Smith was undoubtedly a great help and comfort to the rapidly aging Joseph F. Smith. Father and son often traveled together. One of the last trips they took together occurred in 1914, when the pair traveled in a private railway car throughout the Southern States and the American Midwest. In Independence, Missouri, the Prophet dedicated a new chapel, and father and son called on their cousin, Joseph Smith, III, the son of the founding Prophet, who was then president of the Reorganized Church.

In his capacity as personal secretary to the Prophet, Joseph Fielding Smith met daily with his father and conferred with him on the most sensitive matters involving Church administration. A few days before his father's death on November 19, 1918, he recorded Joseph F. Smith's vision of the redemption of the dead, which is now known as Section 138 of the Doctrine and Covenants.

It is touching to think of these two, working side by side during these years. The venerable Prophet, Joseph F. Smith, who had personally known the Prophet Joseph Smith, and the young Apostle, Joseph Fielding Smith, who would live to preside over the Church in the age of space travel.

"THEY BUILT A NEW FAMILY HOME ON DOUGLAS STREET"

Following his call to the Apostleship, Joseph and his second wife, Ethel, lived in a small house in Salt Lake City, but soon purchased a large lot on Salt Lake's east bench. There in 1925, they built a new family home on Douglas Street to accommodate their growing family of ten children. There were, of course, Josephine and Julina, the two daughters of Joseph's deceased first wife, Louie. Then by the time the family moved into their new house, his second wife Ethel had given birth to eight additional children: Emily, Naomi, Lois, Joseph, Amelia, Lewis, Reynolds, and Douglas.

The new house on Douglas Street had ample bedrooms for all of the children and also space outdoors for the children to play. Since Joseph was an active father who loved sports, the new home had a large lawn, a tennis court, horseshoe pits, and other athletic equipment for the children (and their father) to enjoy. Two years after moving into the new home, an eleventh and final child was born: Milton (whose nickname was "Mitt").

President Joseph Fielding Smith was always very loving and kind toward his eleven children. He never saw one of his children or grandchildren but that he gave them a kiss.

I had the blessing of being personally acquainted with four of the sons of President Joseph Fielding Smith: Joseph Fielding Smith, Jr., Lewis Smith, Reynolds Smith, and Douglas Smith. His relationship with each of these sons reveals much about his character.

"A Lesson on the Word of Wisdom"

When I was younger, I often played golf with President Smith's son, Reynolds Smith, whom we always called "Reyn." Reyn once told me that when he was a student at Roosevelt Junior High School, he had a friend who brought a package of cigarettes to school one day and persuaded Reyn to "try just one puff." When school ended the boys went to an out-of-the-way cul-de-sac near the Junior High, where they thought no one would be watching. They each took a cigarette, lit it with a match, and began to smoke. Reyn told me that at that precise moment a car drove up the cul-de-sac. It was President Smith! Reyn said that he rolled down the car window and said, "Reynolds," a name he used only rarely. "I want to talk to you tonight when you get home!" He then drove away. Reyn fretted over his transgression the rest of the day and finally had the courage to return home for dinner. Not a word was spoken during the meal, but afterwards President Smith invited his son into his study for "a lesson on the Word of Wisdom." Afterwards, President Smith exacted a promise from Reyn that he would never again smoke a cigarette as long as he lived, a promise which Reyn kept.

"AN IMPROMPTU SERMON ON THE EVILS OF PROFANITY"

President Smith fully supported his sons in all of their athletic endeavors. When in the city, he always went to watch athletic events in which his sons were competing, and he did not allow his Church duties to interfere. Douglas Smith, President Smith's youngest son, was a fellow member of the Bonneville Stake, and served as my counselor in the stake presidency during the time that his father presided over the Church. Douglas played football for East High School, which was not far from the Smith home. He told me that his father always came to watch him play football when the Apostle was in town. On one occasion, Doug was injured early in the game. At halftime, the players went into the locker room, carrying Doug with them. President Smith was watching in the stands and made his way to the locker room to check on his son's condition. Doug was lying on the floor of the locker room when his father entered, just in time to hear the football coach, Mickey Oswald, deliver an impassioned halftime exhortation to the players. Doug said that Coach Oswald was angry, and was using "boatswain master's language" laced with mild profanity. Hearing the rough language, President Smith delivered an impromptu sermon on the evils of profanity and the merits of circumspect speech. Meanwhile, Doug pretended to be unconscious on the floor to avoid the embarrassment of facing his teammates and his coach.

"Let's Go Up and Watch the Football Game"

Of all of President Joseph Fielding Smith's sons, Mitt Smith was perhaps the most athletically gifted. Mitt played quarterback on the University of Utah football team. President Smith would attend every home game possible, always arriving early and sitting on the east side of Ute (later Rice-Eccles) Stadium on the University of Utah campus. He was an avid fan and knew all the ins and outs of the game and was not above standing on his feet with the other partisan fans to yell his protest of a bad call.

President Marion G. Romney, who for decades served with President Smith as a member of the Quorum of the Twelve, told me this illuminating story: One General Conference, the University of Utah was playing a football game at Ute Stadium during the Saturday evening priesthood session of Conference. Before the session, President Smith came up to President Romney on the stand in the Tabernacle, leaned over and whispered to him, "Marion, let's go up and watch the football game." President Romney told me that he declined, because he had his young son George with him in the Tabernacle, and did not want to set a bad example for him. President Romney told me that after the opening song and prayer, and when the Tabernacle lights were dimmed for the first speaker, Joseph Fielding Smith slipped quietly out of the Tabernacle to go alone to Ute Stadium to see his son play football.

There are doubtless those who would criticize him for leaving General Conference to watch a football game, but I tend to think President Smith had his priorities absolutely right in this case. President Smith was always a father first.

"A WIDOWER FOR THE SECOND TIME"

Joseph Fielding Smith's second wife, Ethel, was a woman of intelligence and substance and served on the Relief Society General Board for many years. Because Louie's daughters were older, they took responsibility around the home when Ethel traveled on Relief Society business, or when she accompanied her Apostle husband on his ecclesiastical duties. One such trip took Joseph and Ethel on an extended tour of the Central States Mission, including visits to Church history sites in Missouri and Illinois. Joseph and Ethel also took vacation trips with their eleven children.

Beginning in the 1930's, Ethel Smith began to suffer from a debilitating illness and despite all the best medical care available, many priesthood blessings, and the fervent prayers of her family and the Saints, she passed away in 1937. Thus, the Prophet was a widower for the second time, at age sixty-two.

"THEIR UNUSUAL COURTSHIP"

Several of the younger children still lived at home at the time of the death of their mother, Ethel Reynolds Smith, which placed a great burden on the sixty-two-year-old Apostle.

As in the case of the death of his first wife, Louie Shurtliff Smith, Joseph felt that it would be unwise to delay remarriage, and he began courting Jessie Evans, a well-known contralto who sang with the Mormon Tabernacle Choir. My dear friend, David W. Evans, served in the bishopric of the Garden Park Ward, where President Smith lived at the time of Ethel's death. He told me that when Sister Smith died, he stopped by the home to offer assistance. At first, President Smith declined any help, but then he thought and said, "Oh, there is one thing you might do. Will you ask Jessie Evans to sing a number at the funeral?" David Evans told me jokingly that he has since taken credit for having brought President Smith and Jessie Evans Smith together.

Jessie Evans, who was a quarter of a century younger than Joseph, had never married and worked as the Salt Lake County

Recorder. Having decided to court Jessie Evans, Joseph proceeded with caution and tact. Their unusual courtship was a charming interlude, which revealed much about their personalities. Joseph first needed to create an excuse to speak with Jessie Evans, and so one day he called her from the Church Historian's Office. She answered the phone in the Salt Lake County Clerk's Office. He told her that he was prepared to help her to fill gaps in the records of the County with information from the Historian's Office. This led to a series of meetings, which Jessie unromantically referred to as "interviews." Eventually the couple went on various social outings together, some of which included Joseph's eleven children. They were sealed in the Salt Lake Temple by Church President Heber J. Grant on April 12, 1938.

Jessie Evans Smith had been the sole support of her widowed mother for many years, and Mother Evans moved into President Smith's house on Douglas Street after Jessie's marriage to President Smith. In addition to providing her a home, this allowed Mother Evans to care for the younger Smith boys when President Smith and Jessie Evans Smith traveled together on Church assignments.

"Fun-loving and Full of Life"

Jessie Evans Smith, the Prophet's third wife, was always known as "Aunt Jessie" to the family and close associates. Aunt Jessie was a *bona fide* character. She was fun loving and full of life and jokes. She was not averse to telling a ribald joke if the urge struck her—and it struck quite often. Example: "The fruit which brought about the expulsion from the Garden of Eden was not the apple in the tree but the pear ('pair') in the grass." She was a first-rate singer and performed with the Tabernacle Choir for almost fifty years. She enjoyed the limelight immensely and never lost an opportunity to bask in it. President Smith's private secretary, Arthur Haycock, remarked that Jessie Evans Smith seemed determined to "gather the rosebuds while she may."

"AWAKENED BY THE SOUND OF JACKBOOTS"

In 1939 President and Sister Smith left Salt Lake City to tour missions in Great Britain and Europe. They visited all the missions in Great Britain, Scandinavia, and Europe. As the tour progressed, the news of impending war grew increasingly ominous. While in Florence, Italy, on July 4, they were awakened by the sound of jackboots as Mussolini's fascist brownshirts marched directly beneath their hotel window. They then traveled to Germany and were in the country on August 23 when Germany signed a non-aggression pact with the Soviet Union. War was imminent between Germany on the one side and Great Britain and France on the other. The First Presidency responded by ordering the evacuation of all missionaries from Germany. President Smith went to Copenhagen, Denmark, where he oversaw the removal of all missionaries to safety. President and Sister Smith finally returned to the United States in November, after seven months abroad.

"Bowed down with grief"

One of the Prophet's greatest trials and sorrows was the death of his son, Lewis Smith, who was killed in action during World War II.

After the Japanese attacked Pearl Harbor in December of 1941, it became apparent that President Smith's sons might be called up for military duty, as several were eligible to be drafted. The President's son, Lewis, was the first and became a pilot. Douglas and Reynolds soon followed, joining the Army and Navy respectively.

In January of 1944, the family received the shocking word that Lewis had been killed while flying his plane in North Africa. He had flown to India on military business, returned via Palestine, where he had spent Christmas in Bethlehem, and then, as his plane flew over North Africa, it inexplicably exploded in mid-air. He was buried with military honors in Nigeria, the body later being transported and reburied in Salt Lake City. President Smith took great comfort in knowing that his son was a faithful Latter-day Saint to the end.

I was personally acquainted with Lewis, who was stationed near Mobile, Alabama, during his training as a pilot. He was a fine-looking, spiritual, and quiet young man who was called upon often to speak to the Saints. He had a powerful way of preaching and surely would have developed into one of the Lord's great leaders, had he lived. Shortly after I met him, he was deployed to North Africa.

One of the Prophet's sons-in-law, Hoyt Brewster, told me later that if any father could be said to have a favorite son, Lewis was the favorite of Joseph Fielding Smith. Hoyt told me that he had never seen the Prophet so bowed down with grief as he was upon learning of his son's untimely death during the war.

"PHYSICALLY VIGOROUS AND ACTIVE"

In 1950 President Smith became Acting President of the Quorum of the Twelve, and then President in 1951. One of his major labors in this period was the direction of the missionary work. As he approached his eightieth birthday, he was as physically vigorous and active as a man half his age. He made numerous international trips for the Church, touring the Orient, Europe, England, and the United States.

At home, President and Sister Smith sold the old family home on Douglas Street and moved into the Eagle Gate Apartments, less than a block from his office in the Church Administration Building.

"As Excited as a Schoolboy to be Flying"

President Joseph Fielding Smith was always very enthusiastic about flying. Though he was born a generation before the Wright brothers' first powered flight in 1903, he was always interested in the latest advancements in airplanes, jets, and spacecraft. Though he never obtained a pilot's license, he frequently asked for the privilege of sitting in the cockpit of grounded aircraft. He always found air travel exhilarating. He was made an honorary brigadier general in the Utah Air National Guard and became acquainted with several pilots, who often took him on flights in military jet aircraft.

I was with him during a trans-Atlantic air trip to England and back in 1971. Though he was then about ninety-five years old, he was as excited as a schoolboy to be flying in a magnificent jet across an ocean.

President Howard W. Hunter told me this charming story about President Smith's love for flying: In contrast to the President's love of airplanes and flying, President J. Reuben Clark hated flying. President Clark, who served in the First Presidency for nearly thirty years, was adamant against flying and would do anything he could to take alternate transportation. One day President Smith played a good-natured joke on President Clark. President Smith invited President Clark to the airport to inspect a new airplane. Standing on the tarmac, admiring the wings and fuselage, President Clark asked, "What does it look like inside, a boxcar?" To that point in his life, President Clark had never flown in an airplane. President Smith invited President Clark inside to satisfy his curiosity. President Clark was then induced to occupy one of the seats, and just for the experience, to buckle up. When he was securely belted in, President Smith gave a prearranged signal, whereupon the flight crew fired the engines up, and the plane took off with its unwilling passenger.

"MY FIRST IMPRESSIONS OF THE PROPHET"

I first met President Joseph Fielding Smith in April of 1970 when I was called as the secretary to the First Presidency. I still remember my first impressions of the Prophet. He was the first Church President whose father had also served in that position. At nearly ninety-four years of age, he was also the oldest man in the history of the Church to become its President.

President Smith carried a spirit of peace and contentment about him. He was never hurried and did everything with calmness and deliberation. He was of average height, with white hair, a slightly bent posture, and a somewhat shuffling gait. But his handshake was very strong, his memory was clear, and his mentality vibrant and active.

Even in his nineties, he was in remarkably good physical condition. He was quite robust and in excellent health, although, like virtually all persons of his age, he had minor episodes of forgetfulness and occasionally repeated himself, especially when he was tired. He needed a helping hand from time to time, but he came to the office every day. He walked to various meetings in the Church Administration Building and in the temple under his own power. For his age, his strength physically and mentally was a miracle.

It was a great matter of interest to me and even of inspiration to me to discover that his tendency to repeat himself never occurred either when he prayed or when he ordained or set anyone apart. It was truly remarkable, that on those special occasions, the President was magnified in such a powerful way. This was especially true when he ordained Elder Boyd K. Packer as an Apostle in April of 1970. President Smith did not repeat himself once during the lengthy ordination blessing.

In contrast to President Smith, his two counselors, President Harold B. Lee and President N. Eldon Tanner, were relatively young and physically vigorous men in their early seventies. Because of the confidence he had in his counselors, President Smith made broad delegations of administrative authority to them. They handled a myriad of details, freeing the President to provide a steady, guiding presence. President Smith attended all the meetings of the Brethren and was kept apprised about all aspects of the work, retaining the ultimate authority, with the attendant power to revoke his delegations at any time he elected.

"CONSTANTLY PRAYING WITHIN HIMSELF"

After observing President Joseph Fielding Smith for nearly two years, I frequently had the impression that he was constantly praying within himself. There was something about his demeanor that spoke of a man of faith. He was a man of prayer, as were his father Joseph F. Smith and grandfather Hyrum Smith before him, as well as his great-uncle, the Prophet Joseph Smith. All of these great men solved every problem of life through profound and fervent prayer.

"One of the kindest men I have ever known"

President Joseph Fielding Smith was one of the kindest men I have ever known. This was interesting, because in his public ministry he always portrayed an image of sternness, of aloof rigidity, of taciturnity. Because of his apparent solemn, unsmiling demeanor at the pulpit, President Smith projected a serious, unbending, mirthless image to the Church. He had a reputation in the Church for being rather austere in his preaching and in his prolific doctrinal writing. When he conducted a meeting, everything was on the dot; the meeting started on the minute, and there was no question but that Joseph Fielding Smith was in charge. But this image of a cold, stern leader with little patience for the sinner was so at variance with his everyday personality. Behind the scenes, he was a very loving, compassionate man with a wry sense of humor. He never greeted one of his grown sons but that he embraced him and kissed him on the cheek. He was kind. He was humble. He had a sweet, warm, and forgiving nature.

The First Presidency is the ultimate council of resort in the Church, and during President Smith's presidency I sat with him on countless occasions when he considered appeals from disciplinary councils held throughout the Church. There were many tough cases and many sordid cases. I remember him commenting several times, "Why don't people behave themselves!" And yet, after watching him deal with difficult cases of sin or transgression, I was amazed at how merciful and forgiving he was in almost every instance. He showed great compassion and leniency as he decided these appeals. I felt that if I were ever to be judged by a Church tribunal, I would want Joseph Fielding Smith to be its presiding officer!

"A DELICIOUS SENSE OF HUMOR"

There was a delightful, playful side to President Smith. He often exhibited a very keen, exuberant, delicious sense of humor, with an almost puckish quality to it. He was completely without guile or pretension.

Once when meeting with a recently released mission president, the man expressed concern about his ability to complete his report within the allotted time. President Smith responded, "Well, I suppose we can give you an extra minute."

On another occasion, President Smith set apart several brethren to serve in one of the temples. One of them, who was there with his wife, mentioned to the President that he had married them fifty-one years earlier. Cupping his hand and speaking in an aside to the wife, he said, "Can you ever forgive me?"

I was once walking with President Smith and his second counselor, President N. Eldon Tanner. President Tanner observed to the Prophet. "You certainly move along in a spry manner, President." To this President Smith responded, "I should—I've had plenty of practice."

"Watch out! Woman driver!"

President Smith had a sweet relationship with his wife, Jessie. She always had a joke or an anecdote to share. On her kitchen wall hung a placard that announced: "The views of the head of this house do not necessarily represent the views of the management."

When she and the President went in the car, she would always drive. During the years I knew them, they drove a white American Motors Hornet. On one occasion as they were driving away from a chapel where President Smith had spoken, he rolled down his window on the passenger side of the car and called out to a crowd of Saints who had gathered at the curb to wave goodbye. "Watch out," he called in mock alarm. "Woman driver!"

Aunt Jessie had a lovely singing voice and for many years had soloed with the Tabernacle Choir. After their marriage, she would often coax President Smith to sing a duet with her during meetings where they spoke. He invariably referred to these performances as "Do its."

"PRESIDENT SMITH IS HERE!"

President Smith was fond of taking drives with his family in his white Hornet. A special memory in our family is the occasion when the Prophet and Aunt Jessie stopped at our Yale Avenue home while out for an evening drive. My youngest son, Daniel, then about thirteen or fourteen years of age, came running to my study calling, "Dad! Dad! President Smith is here! President Smith is here!" In disbelief, I went outside to find the Hornet parked in our driveway with President and Sister Smith seated inside. After a visit during which all the family members were introduced to the Smiths, they drove on.

"Who is that woman in your office?"

President Smith's office, which was in the northeast corner of the main floor of the Administration Building, was visible from the Smith's apartment. With a small telescope, Jessie could see into her husband's office when the blinds weren't drawn. Once she gazed through the telescope to see a sculptured bust of the President's grandmother, which stood on a pedestal in his office. She promptly called on the telephone, demanding to know, "Who is that woman in your office?"

"THE FIRM HANDSHAKE OF A MAN IN HIS PRIME"

President Joseph Fielding Smith was a lifelong athlete. Even in his nineties he had the firm handshake of a man in his prime. His physical strength was a result of a lifetime of athletic endeavors. One day I walked with him from the Church Administration Building to the Salt Lake Temple. As we walked, he told me that he played handball for many years at the old Deseret Gym. There was a group of four men, the President and three friends, who played weekly. Then, the President told me, when he was in his seventies, he had a life-changing conversation with a medical doctor. President Smith had been playing handball with his usual foursome and was sitting on a bench in the locker room at the Deseret Gym, sweating and puffing from a hard game. A doctor friend walked by and said "Joseph, you're too old to be playing that hard. If you don't stop, you will drop dead on the handball court one day." In response, President Smith asked whether he was recommending that he completely give up the game. The doctor answered, "Yes!" President Smith said to me, "That was the last game of handball that I ever played." We continued to walk towards the Temple for several minutes in silence when he added as a postscript: "And my three friends never forgave me for breaking up the foursome!"

"He never ate meat"

President Smith not only exercised and took care of his body, but he was always very careful with his diet. Towards the end of his life he was also a vegetarian. Although he never told me the reasons for his avoidance of meat, I gained this insight from his personal secretary, D. Arthur Haycock. Arthur told me that the President had an unhappy experience when he was a boy, which led to his avoiding the eating of meat. He was persuaded to go on a rabbit hunt with some of his brothers. On that hunt, President Smith shot his one and only animal. It was a rabbit, and as he walked up to the animal, he found it flopping on the ground and crying, and it seemed to have an accusing expression, as if it were asking, "Why did you do this to me?" He never again killed another animal, and over time began to avoid eating meat. By the time he became President of the Church, he never ate meat.

"A DEEP LOVE FOR THE TEMPLE"

President Smith had a great love for temples, and in particular the Salt Lake Temple. It was a place of great peace for him. He received his endowment in the Salt Lake Temple and was sealed to each of his three wives in that structure. After his son Lewis was killed in action during World War II and following the deaths of his three wives, he retreated to the temple to find solace and comfort. A few months after the death of his son, he was called as the president of the Salt Lake Temple. And of course, as a member of the Quorum of the Twelve and then the First Presidency, he entered the temple weekly for council meetings.

It was while walking to and from the temple with the Prophet that I had some of my sweetest conversations with him.

The temple and temple work always had a central place in President Smith's ministry. In meetings with the counselors in the First Presidency, the Prophet usually deferred to the counselors. They were both much younger men at the top of their game. Both were experienced in Church administration. President Smith knew everything that was going on, but was wise enough to use his two intelligent and able counselors to take the leading oar. He felt no need to be the dominant voice in every matter and was content to let the younger men lead the discussions. The exception was any discussion dealing with the temple. When it came to the temple, his voice was always heard. He had a profound understanding of the temple. He had a deep love for the temple. In all discussions in the First Presidency when the topic of temples came up, he was there, listening intently, directing the discussion, and participating fully with his counselors.

"THE NEXT DAY HE WAS BACK AT HIS DESK"

President Smith had the most remarkable physical strength of any older man I ever knew. He was tough. He was durable. He was strong. A testimony to that fact is that he was never hospitalized during ten decades of life until a few months after he was ordained President of the Church, when he entered the LDS Hospital for tests due to abdominal pain. However, the next day he was back at his desk early in the morning and attended all of his usual meetings.

"A WIDOWER FOR THE THIRD TIME"

President Smith's third wife, Jessie Evans Smith, died while he was serving as the President of the Church, making him a widower for the third time.

It was interesting to observe the Prophet during this time of grief. President Smith was always an outwardly happy man, but those who knew him well understood that he bore many private sorrows. Here was a man who had been married and widowed three times during his long lifetime. The wife of his youth, Louie Shurtliff, died as a young mother in 1908. His second wife, Ethel Reynolds, died in 1937. His third wife, Jessie Evans died in 1971. She preceded the President in death by almost a year, so he was alone during his final months as the President of the Church.

Jessie Evans Smith was only sixty-eight years of age at the time of her passing. Her death came as a great shock to many, as nearly everyone expected that she would survive the Prophet.

"A QUORUM OF LIVING APOSTLES ON FOREIGN SOIL"

A few days after the death of his wife, President Joseph Fielding Smith led a party of General Authorities in attending the first Area Conference to be held in Church history, in Manchester, England. On Friday, August 27, 1971, President Smith attended an historic meeting, held in a conference room in the Piccadilly Hotel in Manchester. It was the first time a quorum of the living Apostles had gathered for a meeting on foreign soil in 130 years! The first such meeting was also in Manchester in 1840. Present in this historic meeting were President Smith; future Church Presidents, Harold B. Lee, Spencer W. Kimball, Howard W. Hunter, Gordon B. Hinckley, and Thomas S. Monson; counselor in the First Presidency, Marion G. Romney; Apostles Richard L. Evans and Boyd K. Packer; future Apostle Russell M. Nelson, and several other General Authorities and others.

"GOD BE WITH YOU, 'TIL WE MEET AGAIN"

At the conclusion of the 1971 Area Conference in Manchester, England, I observed a very touching scene. On the final Sunday, the two final general sessions of the Conference were held at ten o'clock and two o'clock at Kings Hall in Manchester. There was a great outpouring of the Spirit, especially at the end of the last session when the entire congregation remained standing in their places after the Prophet and those with him had left, as if they did not want to leave. Then, spontaneously, the entire assembly burst into song, first singing, "We thank Thee O God for a Prophet," and then, "God Be With You Till We Meet Again." It was a scene never to be forgotten.

In many ways, President Joseph Fielding Smith's participation in the Manchester Conference was a pinnacle of his presidential ministry. After returning to the United States, he often said that it "seemed like a dream." There is no doubt that the Prophet had been magnified and inspired and blessed the lives of many people.

"COMPENSATION FOR A LIFETIME"

President Smith was always unfailingly kind to me, and indeed to all of those who associated with him. A few days prior to the Prophet's death, the Prophet spoke to me as we passed in the hallway. He said, "We certainly appreciate what you do." As he said this, he gave me a friendly pat on the arm. This was almost a compensation for a lifetime!

"HE DIED PEACEFULLY"

On the occasion of the death of Jessie Evans Smith there was a general feeling that the Prophet might not be able to live long without his beloved wife. In the weeks and months following her passing, President Smith seemed quite despondent and even expressed the thought that he ought not to go to Manchester later that month. President Lee and the family ultimately prevailed upon the Prophet to go to England. Meanwhile, the family decided that it would be well for the Prophet to be with one of his children, rather than to live alone in the apartment he had occupied with Aunt Jessie.

In his absence while traveling in England, President Smith's family, at the suggestion of President Lee, moved his clothing and a few of his other personal effects to the home of his daughter and son-in-law, Amelia Smith McConkie and Elder Bruce R. McConkie. There President Smith had a large bedroom and a private bath, which made it more convenient for the family to care for him. The Prophet's oldest son, Joseph Jr., told me that his father had taken the change in good stride and did not appear to be upset by it. To the contrary—he seemed pleased, and a little relieved. President Smith lived comfortably with the McConkies during the remaining months of his life.

On Sunday, July 2, 1972, President Joseph Fielding Smith died quietly at home. He was seated in the same chair in which his wife Jessie died a year before. He had attended sacrament meeting earlier in the day and was chatting with his daughter, Amelia. She stepped out of the room to get something, and upon her return found the Prophet slumped over in the chair.

He died as he lived—peacefully and with no fanfare. He was nearly ninety-six years old.

ABOUT THE AUTHOR

Daniel Bay Gibbons is a writer living in Holladay, Utah. The youngest son of Francis M. Gibbons and Helen Bay Gibbons, he is a former trial attorney and judge and is the author of several previous books. He has served as a full-time missionary, twice as a bishop, and as president of the Russia Novosibirsk Mission.

INDEX

Area Conferences
  Manchester, 11, 76
Argentina, 10
Australia, 10
Beehive House, 35
Benson, President Ezra Taft, 14
Bible
  Smith family, 18
Brazil, 10
Brewster, Hoyt, 55
Carthage Jail, 18
Chicago, 28
Chile, 10
Church Administration Building, 21, 56, 60
Church Historian's Office, 16, 33, 35
Clark, President J. Reuben
  fear of flying, 57
Copenhagen, Denmark, 8, 53
Derby, England, 31
Douglas Street, 7, 17, 41
Eagle Gate, 17
East High School, 45
Ecuador, 10
Edmunds-Tucker Act, 23
England, 5, 9, 30
Essentials in Church History, 7, 34
Evans, David W., 50
Evans, Elder Richard L., 76
First Presidency, 10
Florence, Italy, 7
Garden Park Ward, 50
General Conference, 37
  JFS leaves to watch son play football, 47

Germany, 8
Gibbons, Daniel Bay, 67
Grant, President Heber J., 13
Great Britain, 53
Guatemala, 10
Harrison, U.S. President Benjamin, 25
Hawaii, 25
Haycock, D. Arthur, 52, 71
Hinckley, President Gordon B., 14, 18, 29, 76
Hunter, President Howard W, 14
Hunter, President Howard W., 57, 76
Jenson, Andrew, 33
Kimball, President Spencer W., 76
Kings Hall in Manchester, 77
Kirtland, 18, 20
Lee, President Harold B., 14, 60, 76
Lee, President Spencer W., 14
Little Cottonwood Canyon, 21
Liverpool, 31
London Temple, 9
Lund, President Anthon H., 33
Manchester, England, 11, 77
McConkie, Amelia Smith, 11
McKay, President David O., 10, 29
death, 10
Meg
Smith family horse, 26
Mercy Fielding, 15
Missouri, 10, 15
Mobile, Alabama, 54
Monson, President Thomas S., 14, 76

Mormon Tabernacle Choir, 50
Morrill Anti-Bigamy Act, 23
Morrill Anti-Bigamy Act of 1862, 5
Mussolini, 53
Nauvoo, 15, 18
Nauvoo Legion, 18
Nelson, President Russell M., 76
Nigeria, 54
Nottingham, England, 31
Ogden, Utah, 30
Oswald, Coach Mickey, 45
Packer, President Boyd K., 60, 76
Peru, 10
Piccadilly Hotel in Manchester, 76
Quorum of the Twelve, 47
Quorum of the Twelve Apostles, 6

Relief Society General Board, 49
Reynolds v. United States, 5, 23, 36
Reynolds, Elder George, 36
Reynolds, Ethel, 6
Richards, Elder George F., 9
Roberts, Elder B. H., 33
Romney, President Marion G., 47, 76
Roosevelt Junior High School, 43
Salt Lake City, 17
Salt Lake Stake, 35
Salt Lake Temple, 5, 6, 7, 9, 21, 22, 36, 72
Scandinavia, 53
Shurtliff, Louie, 5
Shurtliff, Louie Shurtliff, 6
Smith, Douglas, 18, 42, 45

Smith, Emma Hale, 15
Smith, Ethel Reynolds, 36, 75
  death, 7, 49
Smith, Hyrum, 15
  trunk belonging to, 17
Smith, Jessie Evans, 7
  background, 50
  courtship, 50
  death, 11, 75
Smith, Jessie Evans, 52
Smith, Joseph Fielding Jr., 29, 42
Smith, Joseph Fielding, Jr.
  son of JFS, 18
Smith, Joseph Richards, 5, 30
Smith, Julina Lambson, 5, 16, 20, 30
Smith, Lewis, 8, 42
  death in World War II, 9
  death of in World War II, 54
Smith, Louie Shurtliff, 30, 75
  death, 35
Smith, Mary Fielding, 18, 20
Smith, Milton, 41
Smith, Milton, 47
Smith, Patriarch John
  son of Hyrum Smith, 29
Smith, President David O., 13
Smith, President George Albert, 9, 13
Smith, President Joseph, 13, 15
Smith, President Joseph F., 5, 6, 13, 20, 21
  death of, 6
  safe belonging to, 17

vision of the
    redemption of
    the dead, 39
Smith, President
  Joseph Fielding
  and Francis M.
    Gibbons, 67
  and Francis M.
    Gibbons, 78
  life
    additional
      counselor in
      First
      Presidency,
      10
    ancestry, 13
    Apostolic
      service, 6, 7,
      8, 9, 34, 38,
      53
    athletics, 69
    attends
      dedication of
      SL Temple,
      22
    birth, 5, 15
    boyhood, 21,
      26
    call to Twelve,
      6, 37
    children, 8, 35,
      41, 43, 45
    church service,
      35
    courtship of
      Louie
      Shurtliff, 30
    death, 11, 79
    death of first
      wife, 6
    education, 27
    employment,
      26, 27, 33
    flying, 57
    home, 7, 35, 56
      Douglas
        Street, 41
    humor, 58, 65,
      66, 68
    love for temple,
      72
    marriage to
      Ethel
      Reynolds, 6

marriage to Jessie Evans, 7
marriage to Louie Shurtliff, 5
mission to England, 5, 30
old age, 59
patriarchal blessing, 29
personal qualities, 59, 62, 63, 78
preaching, 38
President of the Church, 11
President of the Twelve, 9, 10, 56
private secretary to his father, 39
vegetarian, 71
vigor, 74
writing, 7, 33

Smith, Reynolds, 42
and Word of Wisdom, 43
Snow, President Lorenzo, 13, 15
South America, 10
South Pacific, 10
Soviet Union, 53
Swiss Temple, 9
Tabernacle, 48
Tabernacle Choir, 28
Tanner, President N. Eldon, 60
Taylor, President John, 13, 15
Temple Square, 21
The Salt Lake Tribune, 37
U.S. Supreme Court, 5, 23
University of Utah, 47
Uruguay, 10
Utah Air National Guard, 57
Ute Stadium, 47

Whitney, Elder
  Orson F., 33
Woodruff, President
  Wilford, 13, 15, 22
  JFS travels with as a boy, 28
Word of Wisdom, 43

World War II, 8, 54
World's Fair, 28
Wright Brothers, 57
Young Men's General Board, 35
Young, President Brigham, 13
ZCMI, 27

www.ingramcontent.com/pod-product-compliance
Lightning Source LLC
Chambersburg PA
CBHW071312040426
42444CB00009B/1986